Rotters!

John Townsend

Raintree

www.raintreepublishers.co.uk

Visit our website to find out more information about **Raintree** books.

To order:
 Phone 44 (0) 1865 888112
Send a fax to 44 (0) 1865 314091
Visit the Raintree bookshop at **www.raintreepublishers.co.uk** to browse our catalogue and order online.

First published in Great Britain by Raintree,
Halley Court, Jordan Hill, Oxford OX2 8EJ,
part of Harcourt Education.
Raintree is a registered trademark of
Harcourt Education Ltd.

Editorial: Lucy Thunder and Harriet Milles
Design: Victoria Bevan and Bigtop
Picture Research: Melissa Allison and Fiona Orbell
Production: Camilla Crask

Originated by Dot Gradations Ltd.
Printed and bound in Italy by Printer Trento srl

The paper used to print this book comes from
sustainable resources.

ISBN 1 844 21494 X
10 09 08 07 06
10 9 8 7 6 5 4 3 2 1

**British Library Cataloguing in
Publication Data**
Townsend, John
Rotters!: Decomposition
571.9'2
A full catalogue record for this book is available
from the British Library.

Acknowledgements
The publishers would like to thank the following
for permission to reproduce photographs:
Getty/Photodisc pp. 22–23; Harcourt Education
Ltd/Tudor Photography p. 28; Hemera Photo-Objects
p. 28; Holt Images p. 29; Oxford Scientific Films pp.
20–21; Oxford Scientific Films pp. 6–7 (AA/George
Bryce), 16–17 (Mark Turner); Photodisc p. 29; Science
Photo Library/Eye of Science p. 6; Science Photo
Library/Pasieka pp. 10–11; Science Photo Library
pp. 4–5, 28 (Dr. John Brackenbury), 18–19 (Dr Jeremy
Burgess), 24–25 (Pascal Goetgheluck), 8–9 (Eve
Gschmeissner), 14 (E. Gueho), 4, 28 (Astrid and
Hanns-Frieder Michler), 15 (Cordelia Molloy), 16
(Carl Schmidt-Luchs), 6 (David Scharf), 26–27, 29
(Sheila Terry); South Tyrol Museum of Archaeology
pp. 12–13.

Cover photograph of a mouldy plum, reproduced
with permission of Rex Features/Sarah Flanagan.

The publishers would like to thank Nancy Harris
and Harold Pratt for their assistance in the
preparation of this book.

Disclaimer
All the Internet addresses (URLs) given in this book
were valid at the time of going to press. However,
due to the dynamic nature of the Internet, some
addresses may have changed, or sites may have
changed or ceased to exist since publication. While
the author and publishers regret any inconvenience
this may cause readers, no responsibility for any
such changes can be accepted by either the author
or the publishers.

Contents

Some words are printed in bold, **like this**. You can find out what they mean on page 30. You can also look in the box at the bottom of the page where they first appear.

Rotten fruit

It is the first day back at school after the holidays. You open your locker. You step back in horror. What is that horrible smell? What is that buzzing noise? There is something in there – AND IT IS ALIVE!

You peep inside.
Oh no! There are flies buzzing everywhere.
And look! Eeek! A wasp!
And what is that in the corner?
It is an apple. You left it in the locker
before the holiday. Oops!

You reach out your hand…
Ugh! It is all soft and rotten.

Your apple is in a bad way. But don't panic.
It is just rotters at work!

A riddle

Do you think you could change that rotten apple into a nice fresh one? It's possible – but how? The answer is on page 29. But you can read this book and work it out for yourself.

So, what turned your apple rotten?

Little rotters

The rotters that spoilt your apple were tiny creatures called microorganisms. They are called **microbes** for short. **Bacteria** and **fungi** are both microbes.

Microbes are all around us. They are far too small to see. They eat all sorts of things. As they eat, the microbes break food down into a gooey mess. This is called **decomposition**.

Creatures like insects and worms can be rotters, too. This might sound a bit GROSS. But rotters are actually very useful. If they did not make things rot, the world would be piled high with waste!

Three types of rotters:

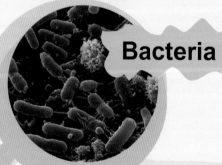

Bacteria

Fungi are ▼ microbes. They often grow on dead or rotten material.

Fungi

▲ Bacteria are microbes. They are very tiny, simple living things. Some of them are rotters, but not all of them. Most bacteria are harmless, but some types can cause disease.

Insects

▼ These creatures are maggots. Maggots are not microbes, but they eat rotting food. When they are fully grown, maggots turn into flies.

So how did the rotters get on your apple…?

bacteria   simple, extremely small microbes
decomposition   breaking down dead material
fungi   plant-like living things that often live on dead or rotting material

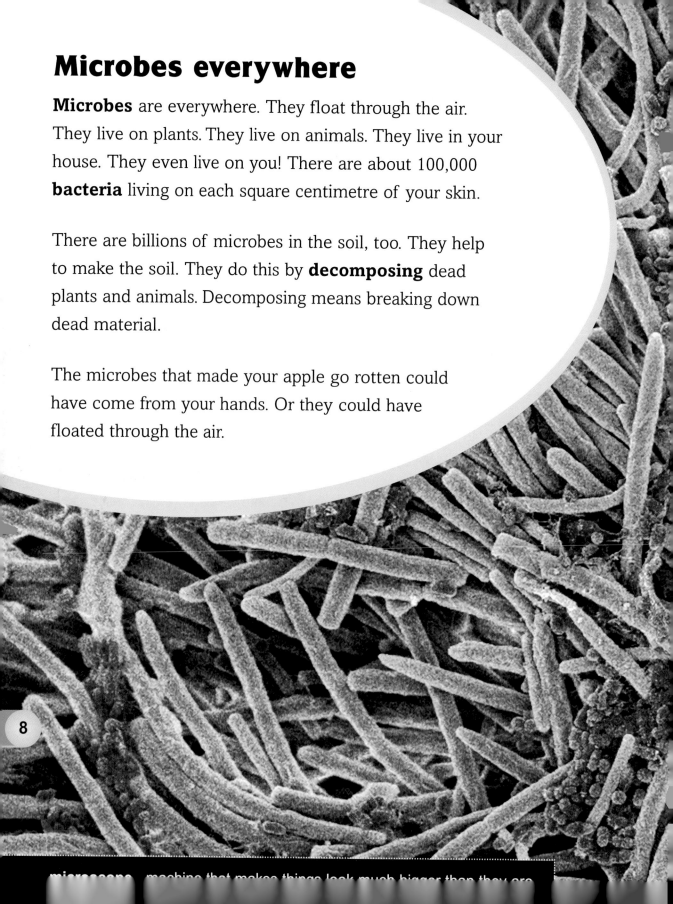

Microbes everywhere

Microbes are everywhere. They float through the air. They live on plants. They live on animals. They live in your house. They even live on you! There are about 100,000 **bacteria** living on each square centimetre of your skin.

There are billions of microbes in the soil, too. They help to make the soil. They do this by **decomposing** dead plants and animals. Decomposing means breaking down dead material.

The microbes that made your apple go rotten could have come from your hands. Or they could have floated through the air.

microscope machine that makes things look much bigger than they are

▼ This is a picture of a person's tongue. It was taken under a **microscope**. The purple clusters are the bacteria. Most bacteria are harmless. Some can make your teeth go bad. So keep brushing your teeth and gums!

Turn the page to find out about the world's smallest rotters

More about bacteria

All **microbes** are tiny, but **bacteria** are even smaller. They can only be seen under a **microscope**. A microscope is a machine that makes things look much bigger than they are.

Bacteria are very tiny. They can feed on things that are too small for us to see. They can live on tiny drops of sweat, or oil on your skin. They might find food in just a grain of dust. A whole apple is a huge feast!

First, bacteria find something to eat. Then they grow and spread until all the food is used up. They eat by oozing juice over the food. The juice **dissolves** the food into a sort of soup. Then the bacteria soak up the soup.

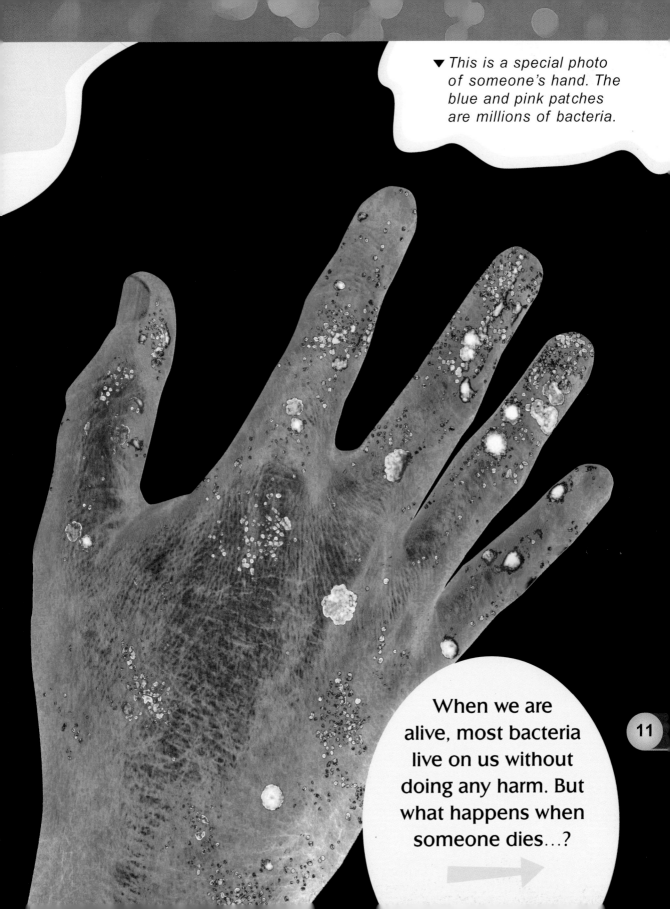

▼ This is a special photo of someone's hand. The blue and pink patches are millions of bacteria.

When we are alive, most bacteria live on us without doing any harm. But what happens when someone dies…?

Rotting bodies

When animals or humans die, their bodies soon begin to rot. Ugh! This sounds horrible! But without **decomposers**, we would never get rid of dead bodies.

As soon as a body dies, **bacteria** start to eat it from inside. Slowly the body rots into the ground.

Bodies decompose faster if the temperature is warm or hot. Bacteria grow very slowly when it is cold. Freezing cold temperatures almost stop the rot.

In 1991, scientists found the frozen body of a man. The body was in the mountains in Italy. He looked as though he had died only a few months before. He had actually been dead for over 5000 years!

Rotten fact!

If the police find a dead body, they can work out how long the person has been dead. They do this by looking at how much the body has decomposed.

decomposer animal or microbe that breaks things down

▼ Scientists called the body from the ice 'Ötzi the iceman'.

13

But some rotters still work in the cold. Just look in your fridge…

Mould

A fridge is not cold enough to stop some **decomposers**.
Food left in the fridge for too long will start to grow **mould**.

There are all kinds of different moulds. Some grow on food.
Others grow on plants. Unlike **bacteria**, moulds can grow
slowly in the cold. They grow really well in the damp.

Moulds are **fungi**. They spread by making **spores**.
Spores are like tiny seeds. They can spread on the
slightest breeze. The spores grow into more moulds.
The green, furry covering you often see on
mouldy food is made of growing spores.

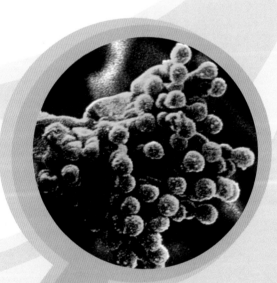

The round balls in this ▶
microscope *photo are*
spores. They grow on
tiny stalks.

mould   kind of fungus that grows on old food and rotting material
spore   tiny 'seed' that can grow into a new fungus

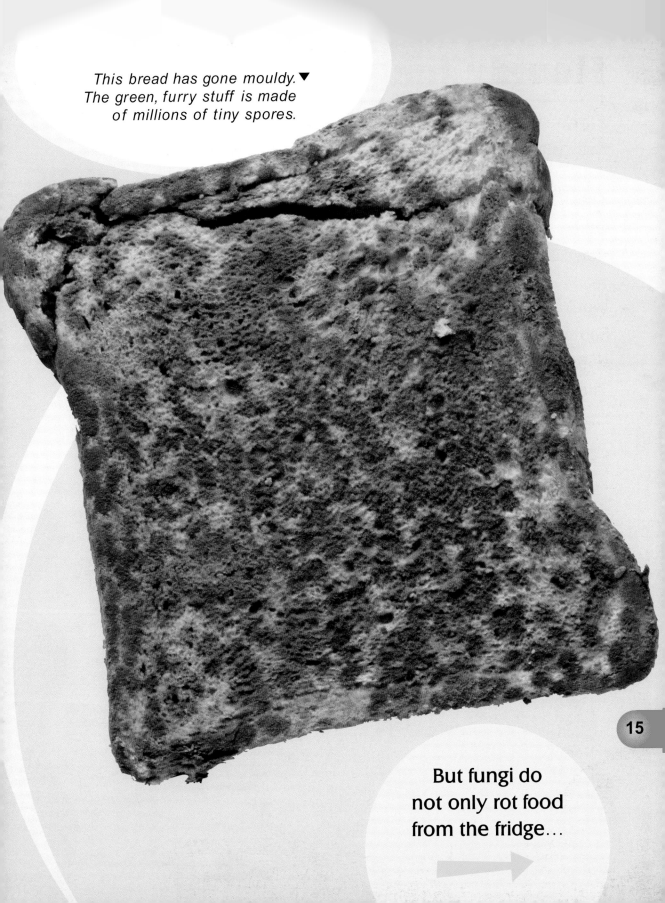

*This bread has gone mouldy.▼
The green, furry stuff is made
of millions of tiny spores.*

But fungi do
not only rot food
from the fridge…

Hungry fungi

Fungi are also **decomposers**. They don't just rot food. Some fungi can rot solid wood. This can take years. But after a long time, fungi can rot a big tree. They can turn it into a crumbly powder!

Fungi "eat" like **bacteria**. They pour special juices over the material they are growing on. The juices **decompose** the material into a liquid "soup". The fungi soak up the soup.

Fungi can also cause diseases that make living plants die. In the 1840s, a fungus caused a plant disease in Ireland. The disease was called potato blight. Many Irish people depended on potatoes for food. The potatoes were ruined by the blight. A million people starved to death.

Rotten fact!

*One fungus that grows on rotting wood is the stinkhorn fungus. The stinkhorn really does stink! It smells like rotting flesh. The smell attracts flies, which spread the stinkhorn's **spores**.*

▼ *Tree fungi can rot solid tree trunks.*

Turn over to
meet some
bigger rotters…

Insect rotters

After a while, **mouldy** and rotting food begins to SMELL. The smell sends out a signal to flies and other insects.

Yum! Flies love to eat rotting food! They can sense that something is rotting from a long way off. Wasps will come too – especially if there is anything sweet around. Wasps love sweet stuff.

Flies also lay their eggs in rotting food. When the eggs hatch, tiny white "worms" called maggots crawl out. As the maggots crawl out, they start to eat the rotting food. In time, the maggots turn into adult flies.

Rotten fact!

*Flies and maggots cannot eat solid food. Instead they spit juice all over what they eat. This **dissolves** solid food into a 'soup'. Then they slurp up the liquid soup.*

▼ Flies can lay up to 250 eggs at a time.

eggs

Some insects eat worse things than mouldy food…

The smelly world of dung

Without all the little rotters around, the world would be piled with dung! Dung is the solid waste that animals make. Many kinds of insects and worms eat dung. Tasty!

Bacteria start to break down the dung inside an animal's body. This is what makes dung smell. Then, splat! The dung hits the ground. The smell of the dung attracts flies. Thousands of them. They swarm on to the dung to lay their eggs.

Dung beetles are another bunch of dung-eaters. They gather fresh dung into balls. Then they roll the dung balls into their underground nests. The female dung beetle lays an egg in each dung-ball. She covers them all over with soil. When the baby beetles hatch, their food is a nice, juicy dung ball!

Rotten fact!

Before 1788 there were no cows in Australia. Then cattle farms were started. Soon there was dung everywhere. It attracted too many flies. So dung beetles were brought in from Europe and Africa. They got to work eating the dung. This helped to solve the problem.

▼ Dung beetles roll balls of dung to feed their young.

Where can you find billions of rotters?

All rotting together

Rotters are good for the soil. Most dead plants and animals end up in the soil. So does rotten food and dung. These things are often full of **bacteria** and other **microbes**. When they reach the ground, billions of rotters come to feed on them. They **decompose** the material into the soil.

Worms are important decomposers. They drag dead leaves and other rotting material below ground. Then they eat them. Then the worms make waste. Their waste mixes into the soil. This makes the soil richer.

Bacteria and other microbes in the soil feed on the worm waste. They make their own wastes, too. This waste is full of good material called **nutrients**. These nutrients help plants to grow strong and healthy.

Rotten fact!

One teaspoon of soil can contain over a billion microbes. There are tiny insects, grubs and worms in there, too.

nutrient food that is necessary for health and growth

▼ *Worms tunnel through the soil, chewing up fallen leaves and animal remains.*

Turn over to find how rotters can save lives....

Using rotters

Rotters can be useful for other things besides **decomposing** dead material. Doctors use them every day to save lives.

Harmful **bacteria** can get into **wounds**. They can rot flesh. This can make people ill. Long ago, doctors found that flies laid their eggs in bad wounds. When the eggs hatched, maggots came out and ate the rotten flesh and bad bacteria. Then the wounds began to heal.

Mould can save lives, too. In 1928, a scientist called Alexander Fleming was studying bacteria that made people ill. He found mould growing in a dish of harmful bacteria. The mould had stopped the deadly bacteria from growing.

This was an important discovery. It helped scientists to use mould to make new drugs. These drugs are called **antibiotics**. Now doctors use antibiotics to fight diseases.

*Maggots like these ▶
are used in hospitals
to clean bad wounds.*

antibiotic drug that kills harmful bacteria that can cause disease
wound cut or other injury to the body

Rotting in cycles

Rotting goes around in a cycle. Animals eat plants, which grow in the soil. The animals drop dung on the soil. Rotters turn the dung into rich **nutrients**. When animals die they rot into the soil, too.

The same happens to dead plants. **Decomposed** plants form a material called **compost**. Compost is full of nutrients. It makes the soil richer. The plants' roots feed on the nutrients in the rich soil. Soon animals eat the new plants. Then the rotting cycle starts again.

Making compost

Did you know that you can make your own compost? You can do this by building a compost heap in your garden. A compost heap is a pile of garden waste and kitchen scraps. Rotters eat away at the pile of waste. After a time, the rotters turn the waste into rich, crumbly compost.

compost   material made from rotted plants

▼ Gardeners often turn dead plants and kitchen waste into brown crumbly compost. They mix it into the soil to feed growing plants.

Apples from apples

What happened to that rotten apple from your locker?
How could it turn into a nice, fresh apple?

The answer is **decomposition**,
and it happens like this:

1

Rotters attack!
- **Bacteria**
- **Fungi**
- Maggots
- Wasps

rotten apple

fresh apple

5

The tree uses the
nutrients to grow a
nice, fresh apple.

2

Apple goes on **compost** heap.

compost heap

3

More rotters get to work!

rich, brown compost

4

Compost is dug in around apple tree.

Apple tree, growing a new crop of apples

Glossary

antibiotic drug that kills harmful bacteria that can cause disease. The first antibiotic discovered came from mould. It was called penicillin.

bacteria simple, extremely small microbes. Many microbes cause waste material to rot. Some bacteria cause disease.

compost material made from rotted plants. Compost makes the soil richer. Plants grow really well in compost because it is so full of nutrients.

decomposer animal or microbe that breaks things down.

decomposition breaking down dead material. This could be dead plants or dead animals.

dissolve break down solid material into a liquid.

fungi plant-like living things that often live on dead or rotting material. We can eat some fungi, such as mushrooms.

microbe creature that is too small to see. You need a microscope to see a microbe.

microscope machine that makes things look much bigger than they are. A strong microscope is needed to see microbes.

mould kind of fungus that grows on old food and rotting material.

nutrient food that is necessary for health and growth.

spore tiny 'seed' that can grow into a new fungus.

wound cut or other injury to the body.

Want to know more?

Books to read

- *Magic School Bus Meets The Rot Squad: A Book About Decomposition*, Linda Ward Beech (Scholastic, 1995)

- *Maggots, Grubs, and More: The Secret Lives of Young Insects*, Melissa Stewart (Millbrook Press, 2003)

- *What is Fungus?*, D.M. Souza (Franklin Watts, 2002)

Websites

- Peep at this… if you dare!
  http://yucky.kids.discovery.com

- For quizzes, microbes in the news, and experiments:
  http://www.microbe.org/index.html

- For lots on fungi:
  http://www.virtualmuseum.ca/Exhibitions/Mushroom/English/index2.html

World's Worst Germs is about microbes that cause disease. These microbes are real rotters!

Rotting is the last stage in a food chain that starts with plants. Find out more in *Shark Snacks*.

Index